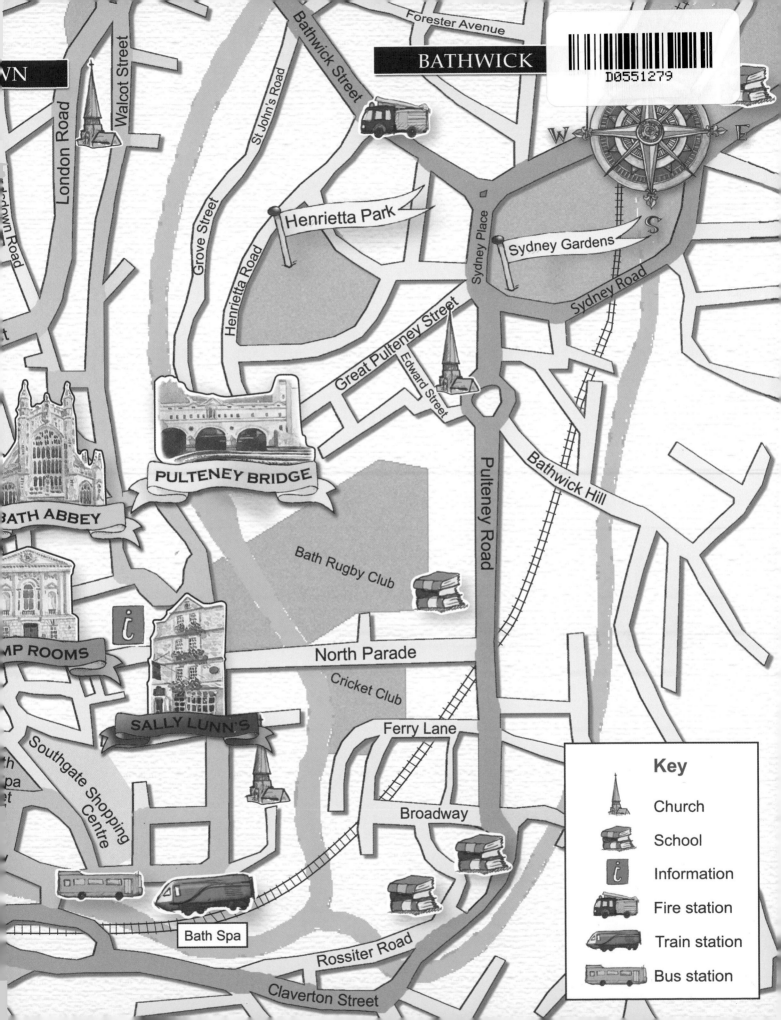

Bath Abbey
Pump Rooms
Pulteney Bridge
The Royal Crescent
The Lawn
Theatre Royal
Assembly Rooms
Green Park
Sally Lunn's

HOMETOWN HISTORY
BATH

My name is Jane Austen. Read about me on page 19.

I am a foot soldier in the Roman Legion. Find out about me on page 4.

JANE WALKER

HOMETOWN WORLD

How well do you know your town?

Have you ever wondered what it would have been like living in Bath when the Romans arrived? What about rubbing shoulders with the finest people in the land in the Assembly Rooms? This book will uncover the important and exciting things that happened in your town.

Want to hear the other good bits? You will love this book! Some rather brainy folk have worked on it to make sure it's fun and informative. So what are you waiting for? Peel back the pages and be amazed at what happened in your town.

Timeline shows which period (dates and people) each spread is talking about

THE FACTS

The Romans are Coming!

A young Celtic shepherd is herding his sheep when he hears an amazing rumble coming from the hillside. As far as he can see, a column of soldiers marches along the valley carrying weapons and knapsacks. Behind them come wagons with women and children. He has never seen such a sight! Why are they here? What do they want? He quickly runs down to the river to warn the villagers working in the fields.

The water might be smelly but it worked miracles for me and Piggy.

This statue of King Bladud can be found in Parade Gardens.

Hot Springs

The Romans invaded Britain in AD 43. They wanted things like grain, iron and gold, as well as cattle and slaves. The Celts had built wooden hillforts at Lansdown and Little Solsbury Hill and were living in the Bath area when the Romans came. The Celts had found the hot-water springs that bubbled out of the ground and threw offerings of coins into the water to please their goddess, Sulis.

A medieval legend tells how a Celtic prince, Bladud, was sent away from his kingdom in 863 BC when he caught a skin disease called leprosy. He became a swineherd and noticed that his pigs' scabby skin improved after wallowing in the mud of the hot springs. When he bathed in the hot springs, his leprosy was cured. Bladud returned home and became king but he never forgot Bath.

Celtic settlements grew up where the River Avon could be crossed easily, such as where Cleveland Bridge now stands. The Romans built the Fosse Way, linking Exeter to Lincoln. The old road runs parallel to the Wellsway, running down Holloway to the city.

Our word 'plumbing' comes from 'plumbum' – the Latin word for lead.

I'll be lucky if I live to see 30! Us Romans have to survive disease and violence!

Sulis Minerva

The Romans also believed the bubbling hot-water springs were the work of the gods. Roman engineers built a huge stone temple and baths around the Sacred Spring. The Romans dedicated the new temple to Minerva, their own goddess of healing and wisdom, as well as to the Celtic goddess Sulis. The Romans then linked Sulis with their goddess Minerva to create a new goddess of the spring, called Sulis Minerva.

A deep stone reservoir lined with lead held the 1.1 million litres of hot water that gushed out of the ground each day – enough to fill over 20,000 bathtubs! Lead pipes carried the water around the baths and are still there, although you can no longer bathe in the original Roman baths because of poisonous lead and bacteria in the water.

The modern spa in Bath today uses natural spring water so that people can enjoy the hot baths once again.

Sulis Minerva was offered gems and coins, many of which are still being found today.

Water flowing from the Sacred Spring is orange because of the iron dissolved in it.

Aquae Sulis

Aquae Sulis is Latin for 'waters of Sulis', the Roman name for Bath. People from across the Roman Empire came to bathe in the baths built around the Sacred Spring for rest and relaxation. They also believed it could cure illnesses. Some visitors were wealthy merchants and pilgrims. Others were wounded soldiers.

Within the town walls, streets were lined with houses, shops, inns and small workshops. Cobblers, plumbers and metalworkers traded and people from the countryside came to sell their goods.

When many Roman troops left Britain in AD 410 to support a rival Emperor back in Rome, Bath had been transformed from a wood and thatch settlement into a stone walled town.

SPOT THIS! Can you spot this statue of King Bladud? Here's a clue: it's by the King's Bath.

AD 43 ROMANS ARRIVE IN BATH...AD 70 TEMPLE AND BATHS BUILT...   ... AD 250 TOWN WALLS BUILT...AD 410 ROMANS LEAVE BATH...

Clear informative text

Hometown facts to amaze you!

'Spot this!' game with hints on something to find in your town

THE EVIDENCE

The Roman baths were a focal point for people. Here, Beric, a young slave boy who works for a Roman merchant, gives his account of a visit to the baths. Beric uses some Latin words in his account. Look at the temple plan to see what they mean.

Yuck! Time to scrape the oil and dead skin from my master's body with a strigil.

Beric's Journal

5th Aprilis AD 200

It was so hot today! I had to stoke the furnace for the hypocaust because my master, Gaius Maximus, complained the caldarium wasn't hot enough. He was in such a bad mood. When we arrived at the baths my master took off his toga and actually threw it at me, muttering about the thief who stole his purse from the bathhouse last week.

I put his clothes in the locker, and followed him to the warm tepidarium. My master took a quick dip in the pool and then I massaged his body with a soft woollen cloth and perfumed oil. Next, he made his way into the steamy caldarium. Back in the tepidarium I scraped his body using a bronze tool called a strigil.

Afterwards, my master rinsed off in the bathing pool before plunging into the icy frigidarium. He usually swims in the Great Bath but today he visited the Sacred Spring instead. He threw in a curse tablet asking the goddess to find his purse and bring the thief to justice ... or else!

Plan of Roman Baths

- Caldarium (hot room)
- Frigidarium (cold bath)
- Tepidarium (warm room)
- Changing rooms
- Hypocaust (underfloor heating)

Temple Courtyard
Temple
Sacred Spring
Oval Bath
Plunge Pool
Great Bath
Circular Bath
Tepid Pool
METRES

This is a plan of the temple and bath complex in the 4th century.

Go back in time to read what it was like for children growing up in Bath

I GIVE TO THE GODDESS SULIS MINERVA THE THIEF WHO HAS STOLEN MY HOODED CLOAK, WHETHER SLAVE OR FREE, MAN OR WOMAN. THE THIEF MAY NOT BUY BACK THIS GIFT UNLESS HE PAYS WITH HIS OWN BLOOD.

Curses like this one asking Sulis Minerva for help were written in Latin. Over 100 curses have been found in the Sacred Spring.

This is a picture of the Circular Bath in 1890 with a curved roof.

How do we know?

We know a lot about the Romans because of what they left behind. The ruins of the baths have been dug up over time. Also we know about the offerings made to Sulis Minerva because of the curse tablets found.

The temple of Sulis Minerva stood below modern Stall Street, outside the Pump Room. Archaeologists have found fragments of stone which when put together make up an image of the Gorgon – a mythical monster. This would have decorated the top of the temple building. The Gorgon, a symbol of the goddess Minerva, was usually female. But this face has a moustache. Perhaps it is a male version of the Celtic goddess of the spring. The Romans often adopted the traditions and beliefs of people they conquered.

The Gorgon had hair of snakes and could turn people into stone.

Intriguing old photos

Each period in the book ends with a summary explaining how we know about the past

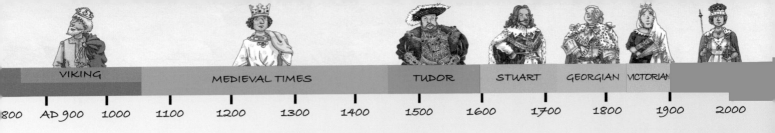

Contents

The Romans are Coming!

A young Celtic shepherd is herding his sheep when he hears an amazing rumble coming from the hillside. As far as he can see, a column of soldiers marches along the valley carrying weapons and knapsacks. Behind them come wagons with women and children. He has never seen such a sight! Why are they here? What do they want? He quickly runs down to the river to warn the villagers working in the fields.

The water might be smelly but it worked miracles for me and Piggy.

This statue of King Bladud can be found in Parade Gardens.

Hot Springs

The Romans invaded Britain in AD 43. They wanted things like grain, iron and gold, as well as cattle and slaves. The Celts had built wooden hillforts at Lansdown and Little Solsbury Hill and were living in the Bath area when the Romans came. The Celts had found the hot-water springs that bubbled out of the ground and threw offerings of coins into the water to please their goddess, Sulis.

A medieval legend tells how a Celtic prince, Bladud, was sent away from his kingdom in 863 BC when he caught a skin disease called leprosy. He became a swineherd and noticed that his pigs' scabby skin improved after wallowing in the mud of the hot springs. When he bathed in the hot springs, his leprosy was cured. Bladud returned home and became king but he never forgot Bath. He helped it to become a great city.

Celtic settlements grew up where the River Avon could be crossed easily, such as where Cleveland Bridge now stands. The Romans built the Fosse Way, linking Exeter to Lincoln. The old road runs parallel to the Wellsway, running down Holloway to the city.

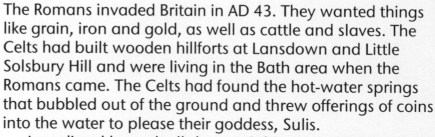

AD 43 ROMANS ARRIVE IN BATH...AD 70 TEMPLE AND BATHS BUILT...

TUDOR
1485-1603

STUART
1603-1714

GEORGIAN
1714-1837

VICTORIAN
1837-1901

MODERN
TIMES
1902-NOW

Sulis Minerva

The Romans also believed the bubbling hot-water springs were the work of the gods. Roman engineers built a huge stone temple and baths around the largest Sacred Spring. The Romans dedicated the new temple to Minerva, their own goddess of healing and wisdom, as well as to the Celtic goddess Sulis. The Romans then linked Sulis with their goddess Minerva to create a new goddess of the spring, called Sulis Minerva.

Sulis Minerva was offered gems and coins, many of which are still being found today.

A deep stone reservoir lined with lead held the 1.1 million litres of hot water that gushed out of the ground each day – enough to fill over 20,000 bathtubs! Lead pipes carried the water around the baths and are still there, although you can no longer bathe in the original Roman baths because of poisonous lead and bacteria in the water.

Our word 'plumbing' comes from 'plumbum' – the Latin word for lead.

The modern spa in Bath today uses natural spring water so that people can enjoy the hot baths once again.

Water flowing from the Sacred Spring is orange because of the iron dissolved in it.

Aquae Sulis

I'll be lucky if I live to see 30! Us Romans have to survive disease and violence!

Aquae Sulis is Latin for 'waters of Sulis', the Roman name for Bath. People from across the Roman Empire came to bathe in the baths built around the Sacred Spring for rest and relaxation. They also believed it could cure illnesses. Some visitors were wealthy merchants and pilgrims. Others were wounded soldiers.

Within the town walls, streets were lined with houses, shops, inns and small workshops. Cobblers, plumbers and metalworkers traded and people from the countryside came to sell their goods.

When many Roman troops left Britain in AD 410 to support a rival Emperor back in Rome, Bath had been transformed from a wood and thatch settlement into a stone walled town.

SPOT THIS!

Can you spot this statue of King Bladud? Here's a clue: it's by the King's Bath.

CELT
500 BC

ROMAN
AD 43-410

ANGLO-
SAXON
AD 450-1066

VIKING
AD 865-
1066

MEDI
TIM
1066

The Roman baths were a focal point for people. Here, Beric, a young slave boy who works for a Roman merchant, gives his account of a visit to the baths. Beric uses some Latin words in his account. Look at the temple plan to see what they mean.

> Yuck! Time to scrape the oil and dead skin from my master's body with a strigil.

Beric's Journal   5th Aprilis AD 200

It was so hot today! I had to stoke the furnace for the hypocaust because my master, Gaius Maximus, complained the caldarium wasn't hot enough. He was in such a bad mood. When we arrived at the baths my master took off his toga and actually threw it at me, muttering about the thief who stole his purse from the bathhouse last week.

I put his clothes in the locker, and followed him to the warm tepidarium. My master took a quick dip in the pool and then I massaged his body with a soft woollen cloth and perfumed oil. Next, he made his way into the steamy caldarium. Back in the tepidarium I scraped his body using a bronze tool called a strigil.

Afterwards, my master rinsed off in the bathing pool before plunging into the icy frigidarium. He usually swims in the Great Bath but today he visited the Sacred Spring instead. He threw in a curse tablet asking the goddess to find his purse and bring the thief to justice...or else!

This is a plan of the temple and bath complex in the 4th century. ➡

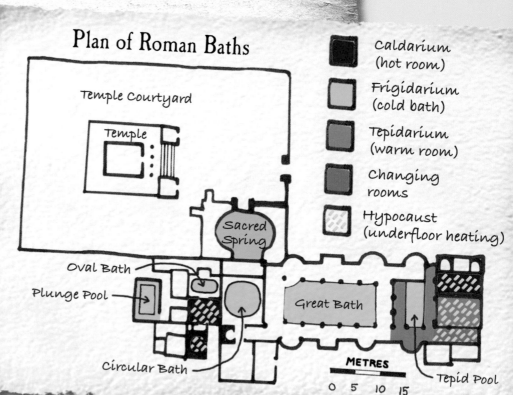

Plan of Roman Baths

Temple Courtyard

Temple

Sacred Spring

Oval Bath

Plunge Pool

Circular Bath

Great Bath

Tepid Pool

METRES
0 5 10 15

- ■ Caldarium (hot room)
- ☐ Frigidarium (cold bath)
- ■ Tepidarium (warm room)
- ■ Changing rooms
- ▨ Hypocaust (underfloor heating)

TUDOR
1485-1603

STUART
1603-1714

GEORGIAN
1714-1837

VICTORIAN
1837-1901

MODERN
TIMES
1902-NOW

This picture shows the Circular Bath with a curved roof in 1890.

I GIVE TO THE GODDESS SULIS MINERVA THE THIEF WHO HAS STOLEN MY HOODED CLOAK, WHETHER SLAVE OR FREE, MAN OR WOMAN. THE THIEF MAY NOT BUY BACK THIS GIFT UNLESS HE PAYS WITH HIS OWN BLOOD.

Curses like this one asking Sulis Minerva for help were written in Latin. Over 100 curses have been found in the Sacred Spring.

The Gorgon had hair of snakes and could turn people into stone.

How do we know?

We know a lot about the Romans because of what they left behind. The ruins of the baths have been dug up over time. Also we know about the offerings made to Sulis Minerva because of the curse tablets found.

The temple of Sulis Minerva stood below modern Stall Street, outside the Pump Room. Archaeologists have found fragments of stone which when put together make up an image of the Gorgon — a mythical monster. This would have decorated the top of the temple building. The Gorgon, a symbol of the goddess Minerva, was usually female. But this face has a moustache. Perhaps it is a male version of Sulis, the Celtic goddess of the spring. The Romans often adopted the traditions and beliefs of people they conquered.

CELT
500 BC

ROMAN
AD 43-410

ANGLO-SAXON
AD 450-1066

VIKING
AD 865-1066

MEDI
TIM
1066-

Bath Coronation

It's a sunny Whitsunday morning. An excited crowd has gathered in the courtyard outside the monastery church of Saint Peter, where Bath Abbey stands today. Suddenly, the crowds hush and turn to watch as the new king and his party emerge from the great wooden door. Dressed in richly coloured robes, his golden crown glinting, King Edgar walks solemnly into the sunlight. It's a great day for Bath – the coronation of the king!

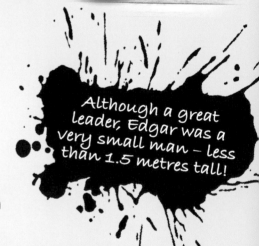

Hail Edgar, first King of England!

Doesn't he look smart!

United Kingdoms

Until Edgar's coronation England was divided into kingdoms. When the Romans left Britain, the Angles and the Saxons invaded from Germany and Scandinavia. In AD 577 the Saxons fought the Britons in the Battle of Dyrham, north of Bath, and won!

Over many years they settled amongst the Britons in the kingdoms of Mercia and Wessex and became known as Anglo-Saxons.

By now, much of Roman Bath lay in ruins. It flooded regularly when the River Avon burst its banks. A new convent was built close to the present Abbey. In AD 781 King Offa built an even bigger abbey church and monastery.

Although a great leader, Edgar was a very small man – less than 1.5 metres tall!

SPOT THIS!

This Victorian stained-glass window in Bath Abbey shows Edgar being crowned by Dunstan, Archbishop of Canterbury.

Almost 100 years later, King Alfred the Great rebuilt the town of Bath on top of the old Roman streets. He built new entrances into the walled town at North Gate and South Gate. The main route through the town led from West Gate across to East Gate and beyond the walls to the mill on the River Avon. Alfred used the old Roman defences to fortify Bath against attack from new invaders – the Vikings.

On 11th May AD 973, Edgar, sometimes called Edgar the Peaceful, was crowned. This was a great event for Bath. Edgar's coronation brought together two kingdoms: Wessex in the south west and Mercia in the Midlands. England was uniting as a country.

8

...AD 577 BATTLE OF DYRHAM...AD 781 OFFA BUILDS NEW ABBEY...

Minted

A woman's skeleton was found buried with monks in the Bath Abbey vaults.

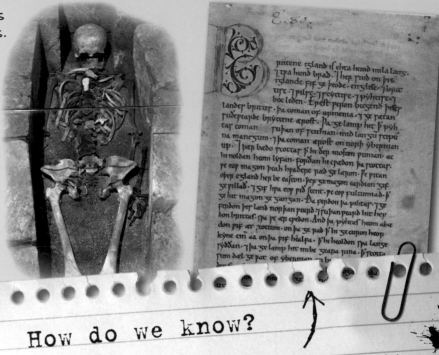

The Vikings came by boat from Scandinavia to raid the wealthy monasteries of Britain around AD 800. In Bath, a mint set up in AD 901 produced fine silver coins. These were used to pay off the Viking raiders to stop them invading. We know this because archaeologists have recently found coins minted in Bath among Viking treasure in Scandinavia.

By the time Edgar was crowned king, Bath was a small, successful market-town, the largest in Somerset. It stood in an important place on the border between the kingdoms of Mercia and Wessex.

Alas, poor Gunnarr. He was brave but unlucky.

Carvings on this Viking stone say: 'Gunnarr, son of Rode, was buried by his brother Helge in a stone coffin in Bath'.

How do we know?

A poem describing Edgar's coronation appears in the Anglo-Saxon Chronicle. The Chronicle is a history of Anglo-Saxon England, hand-written in Olde English by monks. The Battle of Dyrham is also recorded in the Chronicle and Bath is mentioned a few times. Bath at this time was known as Bathon (meaning 'at the baths'), or sometimes Hat Bathu ('hot baths').

Many places in and around Bath still have their Anglo-Saxon name. The Old English word for a hill was 'down', giving us Lansdown (long hill), Odd Down (Odda's Hill) and Claverton Down (hill above the clover place). 'Combe' means 'valley' in Old English. Can you work out what 'Combe Down' means?

CELT
500 BC

ROMAN
AD 43-410

ANGLO-
SAXON
AD 450-
1066

VIKING
AD 865-
1066

MEDIEV
TIMES
1066-14

Monks and Mills

"Come, feel my fine cloth! It's the best you can buy in Bath," the cloth merchant calls to passers-by. The fair is open and Bath is filled with merchants, weavers, spinners, farmers and, of course, monks. The streets are piled high with sacks of wool for sale. There is a rumour that the monastery has just purchased 300 sacks. That should keep the woollen mill busy!

Yippee, market day! We need more wool for our socks.

Rich...

Medieval Bath was at the centre of a thriving woollen trade. The woollen mills were owned by the monastery which, by this time, had become rich and powerful. The monastery and abbey, now Bath Abbey, was a gift to the Norman doctor, John of Tours, from King William Rufus (William the Conqueror's son).

The medieval King's Bath was built between the 12th and 13th centuries and was in use for almost 600 years. You can still visit it today.

John paid the king £500 of silver for the town of Bath, the mint and the hot springs. But by this time the monastery church had burned down. So when John became the first Bishop of Bath, he set about building a new cathedral and palace in its ruins.

...and Healthy

As a doctor, John of Tours was fascinated by the healing power of the hot-water baths. The original Roman roof had long since collapsed, and the bathhouse walls lay in ruins. The King's Bath was built over the lower walls of the original Roman reservoir. Arched seating areas were added to provide shelter for the bathers.

...1088 MONASTERY CHURCH BURNS DOWN...1090 FIRST BISHOP OF BATH...

TUDOR
1485-1603

STUART
1603-1714

GEORGIAN
1714-1837

VICTORIAN
1837-1901

MODERN
TIMES
1902-
NOW

Poor...

Although medieval Bath had a magnificent monastery, abbey and baths, it was also a busy, cramped market town. The poorer townsfolk lived in tiny timber-framed houses along dirty, narrow streets. Most of the town was inside the original Roman walls, but new suburbs were springing up outside the town gates. At the heart of the town was a large open space where local traders set up stalls and pens for their livestock at the weekly market. A brand-new street – Stall Street – linked the centre with South Gate down by the river.

...and Sick

A terrible event brought a sudden end to Bath's wealth and the power of the monastery. In 1348 the Black Death struck, killing around half of Bath's population, including the monks.

People passed through East Gate on their way from the town to catch the river ferry to Bathwick and the woollen mills. The gate can be found below Boat Stall Lane.

Rats everywhere! No wonder the Black Death has spread so fast!

How do we know?

How do we know about the wool market in Bath? In 1284 the Bishop of Bath and Wells received a royal charter from the king, granting him the right to hold a ten-day fair in Bath. The monks had introduced the latest spinning and weaving techniques from France. Bath was famous for its tightly woven broadcloth, made on broad looms. At one time there were as many as 50 broad looms busy at work in one street – the one we now call Broad Street.

The Royal Charter granted the right to hold a ten-day fair in Bath.

Broad Street, named after the broad looms, is one of Bath's narrowest streets!

CELT
500 BC

ROMAN
AD 43-410

ANGLO-
SAXON
AD 450-
1066

VIKING
AD 865-
1066

MEDIE
TIM
106
148

The Abbey Destroyed

The terrified old abbot watches, helpless, as the king's men destroy his precious abbey. They take the coloured glass from the windows and strip lead from the windows and roof. Even the wooden pews are being looted. A sudden clang from above tells the abbot that even the abbey bells are no longer safe. Soon there will be nothing left but an empty ruin. The year is 1539 and the king, Henry VIII, has ordered the destruction of Bath's abbey.

Jacob's ladder on the west front of the abbey represents Bishop King's dream of angels climbing ladders to heaven.

Bishop King's Dream

Bishop Oliver King would have had nightmares if he had seen what was happening to his abbey. When he arrived in Bath in 1499 as the new Bishop of Bath, he was fulfilling a dream. In his dream, God urged him to rebuild the abbey church that the lazy monks had neglected. Bishop King introduced new rules and rebuilt inside the ruins of the old abbey. But his abbey did not survive long.

Henry VIII had fallen out with the Catholic Pope over his divorce from the queen, Catherine of Aragon. Henry made himself head of a new Church of England and set about destroying the monasteries, which were run by Catholic monks. On 27th January 1539 the abbot and his monks in Bath surrendered the abbey and monastery, ending almost 900 years of their rule.

Royal Seal of Approval

When Henry's daughter, Elizabeth I, came to the throne in 1558, Bath was rescued. Elizabeth set aside money to rebuild the abbey. It was to be a parish church dedicated to St Peter and St Paul, and known simply as Bath Abbey.

Elizabeth and her court visited Bath in 1574 to check on the progress of the building work. It was a great occasion! The town's streets were cleaned up and buildings were decorated to welcome the royal party. A choir came from Wells Cathedral and the very first sermon was preached in the new abbey.

TUDOR
1485-
1603

STUART
1603-1714

GEORGIAN
1714-
1837

VICTORIAN
1837-1901

MODERN
TIMES
1902-NOW

Bathers and Beggars

In 1590, Elizabeth I granted Bath the status of a city, and gave its new mayor and councillors the power to make local laws, punish people and put them in prison. Bath was now a fashionable spa resort. New hotels and lodging houses quickly sprang up in the area around the baths.

Visitors enjoyed the newly repaired King's Bath, which now had its own changing rooms. The hospitals of St John's and St Catherine's, built close to the baths, cared for the sick, the elderly and the poor. In 1576 a tiny Leper's Bath was built next to the Hot Bath.

Bath had also attracted beggars. In 1601 a Poor Law was passed which allowed the city council to give idle beggars a good whipping. They were then sent either back to their own village, or to a special 'house of correction'. The Poor Law did provide shelter and work for the deserving poor.

SPOT THIS!
Can you find this rebus (picture puzzle)? When all the pictures are put together they make the name of Bishop Oliver King.
A mitre (bishop's hat), an olive tree and a king's crown.
Here's a clue: it's on the Bath Abbey.

A horse bath was built beyond South Gate to wash the horses that tramped the city's streets!

Neigh, this bath is a bit cold!

Nay, you're just spoilt.

Free School

In 1552, Bath's first school, the Free Grammar School of King Edward VI, was set up in the city centre. Its pupils were all boys between the ages of 7 and 15. They had to pay fees to go to the school – the 'free' in the name meant that the school was open to all boys and free from any restrictions. What was life like in a 16th-century school? Joshua Smith, a 10-year-old pupil, describes a typical day.

Dies Lunae (Monday)

I got to school at 6 o'clock this morning, just as the bell rang. The Master was sitting, as usual, on the raised platform at one end of the classroom. He is so strict! I spoke to him in English instead of Latin and was punished. I was whacked 3 times across my buttocks! Then my stomach started rumbling while we were reading from the Bible. I was glad of my packed breakfast at half-past nine. Then we took turns to read, translating the Greek Odyssey. I ran home for lunch and then back to school. Four more hours I sat on that hard bench with my book on my knees until my buttocks were quite numb. And now I have to do my homework before the light goes!

CELT
500 BC

ROMAN
AD 43-410

ANGLO-
SAXON
AD 450-
1066

VIKING
AD 865-
1066

MEDIE
TIM
1066-

The Battle of Lansdown

It's dusk, and the exhausted soldiers of Sir William Waller's Parliamentarian army have retreated behind a low wall. Before them stretches a grim sight – dead and wounded men and horses lie scattered over the battlefield. The muskets of General Horton's Royalist soldiers continue to fire, making the air thick with smoke and the stench of gunpowder. As darkness falls, the firing stops.

For or Against?

On 5th July 1643, Bath was caught up in the English Civil War. The Parliamentarian army of Oliver Cromwell was in Bath, while the much larger Royalist army, supporting King Charles I, was camped at Wells. The two sides fought a fierce battle on Lansdown Hill. The two commanders had been friends when they were younger. The outcome was not clear, and both sides claimed victory.

At first, the loyal citizens of Bath supported the king in the Civil War, although they weren't happy that he had earlier tried to raise taxes and bring back the Catholic religion. City councillors were also angry about having to provide gunpowder to the king's army, which was garrisoned in the city. An entry in the council records shows an order for gunpowder crossed out. Bath had switched sides and started supporting Parliament instead.

Today a post marks the place where the Battle of Lansdown took place.

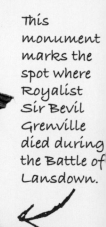

This monument marks the spot where Royalist Sir Bevil Grenville died during the Battle of Lansdown.

TUDOR
1485-1603

STUART
1603-1714

GEORGIAN
1714-1837

VICTORIAN
1837-1901

MODERN
TIMES
1902-NOW

Just my luck to get the bum job!

Dirty...

With the country at war with itself, Bath hadn't changed much from medieval times. It was still a smelly, dirty, crowded town within the old city walls. Rubbish and sewage were emptied onto the streets or thrown over the city walls. Only the residents of Southgate Street were luckier. At the end of each garden was a simple toilet that drained into a ditch and then into the river beyond. The name of the ditch was...Bum Ditch!

...and Clean!

In the 1600s the city appointed a scavenger to collect the rubbish and sewage. By the time the Civil War ended and King Charles II visited Bath in 1668, the town had been cleaned up. Among the royal party was a man called Samuel Pepys. In his diary he says that he was impressed with the city's clean streets. But, after visiting the Cross Bath he adds, "only methinks it cannot be clean to go so many bodies together in the same water".

Men and women bathed together, while spectators threw in the odd dog or cat to liven things up!

A doctor called Thomas Guidott moved to Bath in the same year. He believed that the spa waters could cure illnesses so the spa water was soon being bottled and sold as a miracle cure.

This map shows us what the city was like just over 300 years ago. Can you find where your favourite shop would have been?

How do we know?

The map above was made in 1694 by Joseph Gilmore, a maths teacher from Bristol. It shows the different lodging houses in the city. By the end of the 1600s there were more than 18 inns and 25 lodging houses in Bath. Can you see a bowling green and tennis courts marked on the map?

SPOT THIS!

Sally Lunn arrived in Bath in 1680 but the house where she worked was already old. Sally Lunn's Teashop was one of a row of timbered houses that show us what buildings were like before Georgian Bath was built.

...1668 CHARLES II VISITS BATH...1680 SALLY LUNN ARRIVES IN BATH...

15

CELT 500 BC

ROMAN AD 43-410

ANGLO-SAXON AD 450-1066

VIKING AD 865-1066

MEDIEVAL TIMES
1066-14

Building Bath

The sound of the stonemason's chisel rings out as he sets to work on a new slab of stone. More stone blocks from the quarry have just arrived at the river for loading. The sturdy crane lifts a huge block from the first truck onto the waiting barge. It will take the stone upriver for important new buildings in Bath, Bristol and even London. The horses neigh impatiently as they wait to haul the empty trucks back up the hill to Mr Allen's quarry at Combe Down.

City of Stone

At the beginning of the 1700s about 3,000 people lived in Bath. Within 100 years, Bath had grown into a city with a population of around 30,000! Queen Anne visited in 1702 and 1703 to improve her health. Almost overnight the city started attracting rich visitors seeking cures for their illnesses.

By the time Anne's cousin, George I, became king, there was a shortage of housing. Two local men set about transforming Bath's city centre. One was the stone-quarry owner, Ralph Allen. The other was the architect, John Wood the Elder. His son, John Wood the Younger, became his father's assistant and continued his work when his father died in 1754. The Royal Crescent is one of his most famous designs.

I do hope the baths will cure my sore toe.

This picture, dated 1773, shows John Wood the Younger's newly built Royal Crescent. It was the first crescent-shaped terrace in the world.

...1702 QUEEN ANNE VISITS BATH...1703 THE QUEEN RETURNS...

Ralph Allen

Ralph Allen came to Bath as the local post office clerk and worked his way to postmaster then on to became mayor of Bath. At that time the postal service was slow as all the mail went via London on horseback. Ralph Allen introduced a network of faster cross-country routes and made his fortune.

With his money, Allen bought the stone quarries at Combe Down and had a magnificent estate built for himself at Prior Park (which is now a school). He also built cottages for his stonemasons, and donated money and stone to build the Mineral Water Hospital.

The men who built Bath: from left to right, Richard Jones, Ralph Allen, Robert Gay and John Wood the Elder.

John Wood

John Wood the Elder wanted to re-create the magnificent city of King Bladud. He designed a meeting place, the Royal Forum, an Imperial Gymnasium for exercise and sport, and a Grand Circus for sporting events. Only the last of these three was actually built. His three greatest buildings are Queen Square, where he lived, finished in 1736, Prior Park in 1741 and the Circus in 1754.

SPOT THIS!

Can you find a doorway in the Circus with a monkey carved above it? What other carvings can you spot?

Prior Park and the Palladian bridge, painted by Henry Venn Lansdown. Prior Park was built to show off the qualities of Bath stone.

William Oliver

Bath also attracted a stream of poor and sick people. The large number of visitors coming to drink the mineral waters meant that new facilities were needed. William Oliver, a doctor from Plymouth, encouraged the City Council to build a Pump Room next to the King's Bath, for people to drink the waters in comfort.

Oliver later joined with Ralph Allen and John Wood to build the new Mineral Water Hospital. Patients could make the short journey from the new hospital to the Hot Bath for their treatments, without disturbing the elegant people taking the waters at the Pump Room. In just over 70 years a magnificent new city had been created by local men using local materials.

Georgian Highlife

Inside the ballroom it is very hot. There must be at least 800 people in the Assembly Rooms this evening. Miss Elizabeth has danced three times and now sits fanning herself. Captain Bennet has kindly gone for some lemonade. He is very dashing, especially compared with some of the dandies prancing about the ballroom. Miss Elizabeth's dance card was filled within half an hour of arriving! She will post her dance card to her mama first thing in the morning to show her!

Entertainment

Living in Bath during the Georgian era was an exciting time. Visitors came to take the spa waters, meet friends at the Pump Room or discuss the news of the day at the new coffee houses on North Parade or Milsom Street. A short stroll across the newly built Pulteney Bridge took them to Sydney Gardens where they could enjoy the new swing and maze, or take a ride around the park. There was also a flourishing theatre where the famous actress Sarah Siddons performed.

The best entertainment could be found at the Assembly Rooms. Wealthy people arrived by coach or sedan chair to enjoy grand balls, concerts and card games. Bath soon became the place to be seen during the season when fashionable young ladies were introduced into society. It was a great place for young people to find partners.

You can drink spa water from the King's Fountain in the Pump Room. It's not to everyone's taste, though!

SYDNEY GARDENS
PUBLIC SUBSCRIPTION

for walking one month, each person, 4s.;
for 3 months, 7s. 6d.; and the season, 10s.
If two in one family,
each 7s 6d

This notice tells us how much people had to pay to use Sydney Gardens when it was first opened. 'S' stands for shillings and 'd' stands for pence.

Lower Assembly Rooms

A Welshman called Richard Nash was in charge of social life in Bath from 1705. As the city's Master of Ceremonies he had a strict code of behaviour to make sure events ran smoothly. He inspected new arrivals to see if they were suitable to attend the city's balls and receptions. He banned swearing and carrying swords, and encouraged people from different backgrounds to mix more easily. Nash's extravagant clothes earned him the nickname 'Beau' (French for 'beautiful').

People paid a subscription to go to balls at the Lower Assembly Rooms.

Beau Nash died in poverty with huge gambling debts in 1761. The City Corporation paid for a lavish funeral, but Beau Nash was buried in an unmarked pauper's grave. You can see a memorial to him in Bath Abbey.

There were two popular Lower Assembly Rooms in Bath – Harrison's and Lindsey's. The Lower Assembly Rooms building burnt down in 1821.

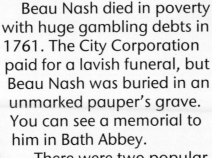

Richard 'Beau' Nash

SPOT THIS!

Beau Nash lived in a fine house next to what became the Theatre Royal in 1805.

'Bog Island' is now where Harrison's Assembly Rooms once stood.

Upper Assembly Rooms

The Upper Assembly Rooms opened in 1771. They were designed by John Wood the Younger. Twice a week, the ballroom attracted 800–1,200 guests. The writer Jane Austen lived in Bath between 1801 and 1806. Though it was not her favourite place, she describes life in Bath in two of her books, *Northanger Abbey* and *Persuasion*. Many celebrities visited Bath Assembly Rooms, including Charles Dickens, the portrait painter Thomas Gainsborough and the composers Haydn and Strauss.

Jane Austen

Kitty is a kitchen maid working in a house in the Royal Crescent. Eliza Tyndall, her mistress, has invited her family to stay for the season. She clearly wants to make a good impression on the visitors. Rooms have to be aired, mattresses turned, silver polished and an extravagant menu prepared. Kitty shares an attic room with Betty, the under parlour maid.

Maybe Cook will let us eat the cold leftovers for supper...

Thursday

The house has been in uproar all week. Mistress Tyndall's niece, Miss Elizabeth has come to stay. And there are to be twelve guests for dinner! Cook was flustered and shouting at all us maids. I spent hours in that dark, damp scullery plucking peacock feathers and scrubbing vegetables until my hands were raw. There were enough to fill two big copper pans. Then Cook asked me to get the leg of lamb ready to go on the spit. Poor Frisky had to go in the wheel today. I hate it when he's in there – it must be so hot and smoky above the roaring coal fire.

Cook made a beautiful peacock pie to go in the centre of the dining table. The mistress and her visitors finally sat down for dinner at 6 o'clock. We were still clearing away when they all went off to the Ball. I've been on my feet since 6 o'clock this morning. It's now almost midnight and Betty keeps telling me to blow out the candle.

Cook's menu

White soup
Poached salmon
Roast mutton
Potato pudding
Cheese
Peacock pie
Whipped syllabub trifle
Nuts and sweetmeats

In Georgian kitchens meat was cooked over the fire on a metal spit. In some houses, a small dog was placed inside a wheel above the cooking range. As the dog ran around, the spit turned and the meat cooked evenly!

How long do I have to keep running to cook a leg of lamb?

A popular way to get around Bath in Georgian times was by sedan chair. A sedan was a chair inside a covered box carried on two long poles by two servants. It meant the wealthy could be carried around in style, without getting their feet wet. Sedan chairs were also good for going to and from the baths. Larger houses had wide entrances so that chairs could be carried up to the next floor.

Sedan chairs were invented by the French.

How do we know?

The post was the only way for people to pass on news or documents such as Miss Elizabeth's dance card. The person who received the letter had to pay the letter carrier. The cost of the letter depended on how far it had travelled and how many sheets of paper were used.

In 1784 the Post Office replaced its post boys on horseback with new horsedrawn mail coaches. The idea came from John Palmer who owned the Theatre Royal in Bath and a theatre in Bristol. He used a coach to move actors and scenery quickly between his theatres. He organised and paid for the first mail coach run from Bristol to London via Bath. It took 16 hours, cutting the time it had taken using post boys by more than half.

The mail coach setting off from Bath, crossing the old bridge.

Poverty and Progress

Some children are playing a game of tag in the street. Two boys kick a ball made of old rags. A small girl with a skipping rope watches a game of marbles being played on the pavement. The children stop playing and run over when the barrel organ appears around the corner. The organ grinder slowly turns the handle and the music starts to play. His monkey dances around on top of the organ. The children are amazed – they have never seen anything like it before.

The slums of Avon Street were dirty and crowded, and often flooded when the nearby River Avon burst its banks. Today, you will find a multi-storey car park there.

A Hard Life

Life was very hard for poor families living in Victorian Bath. Living conditions grew worse as more people moved to the town from the farms and villages to find work. Families lived together in damp, overcrowded houses, often with no running water and surrounded by rubbish and sewage.

Avon Street was one of the worst in Bath. When a cholera epidemic broke out in 1831, more than half of the people who died from the disease were from Avon Street. Poor people were not expected to live very long anyway. On average, a lawyer or doctor in Victorian Bath could expect to live until the age of 55, but a labourer could expect to live only to 25 years old.

The Kennet and Avon Canal

The stone quarries brought more work to Bath, but transporting the stone was a problem. A plan was drawn up to build a canal connecting the River Avon with the River Thames, providing a cross-country route from Bristol all the way to London.

The 100-kilometre long Kennet and Avon Canal took 16 years to build and was completed in 1810. However, the opening of the railway just 30 years later was disastrous for the canal – it could not compete with the much faster railway service.

Horse-drawn carriages wait to collect passengers outside Brunel's new Bath railway station.

God's Wonderful Railway

The Great Western Railway (GWR) was built between 1835 and 1841. It provided plenty of jobs, and labourers' wages rose by 25 per cent. Designed by the engineer Isambard Kingdom Brunel, the railway linked London to Bristol via Bath. It became known as 'God's Wonderful Railway'.

And it was a wonder. Box Tunnel, just outside Bath, was the longest tunnel in the world when it was built. In Bath the roofed railway station brought passengers to the city centre. A second station at Green Park, where Sainsbury's is today, was added later to link Bath with Birmingham and the south coast. The railway line improved Bath's transport links, and soon new factories and foundries were expanding along the nearby Lower Bristol Road.

One hundred workers died building the Box railway tunnel, just outside Bath.

Clear off! No riff-raff allowed!

SPOT THIS!

Can you find this stone obelisk with the young Queen Victoria's face carved on it? It was put up in 1837 to celebrate the queen's 18th birthday. Here's a clue: it's in Royal Victoria Park.

Parks and Baths

By now public parks were being created in the crowded city to provide fresh air and exercise. Bath's Royal Victoria Park opened in 1830. At first visitors had to pay a small entrance fee. Eager park wardens were instructed to remove anyone thought to be dirty or undesirable.

A new hotel, the Grand Pump Room Hotel, opened opposite the Pump Room in 1869, and a new warm-water bath was built. The dressing rooms had their own fireplaces! Before the foundations were built, archaeologist James Irvine dug up the area and found evidence of the Roman baths, including the Temple of Minerva. The hotel was demolished in 1959.

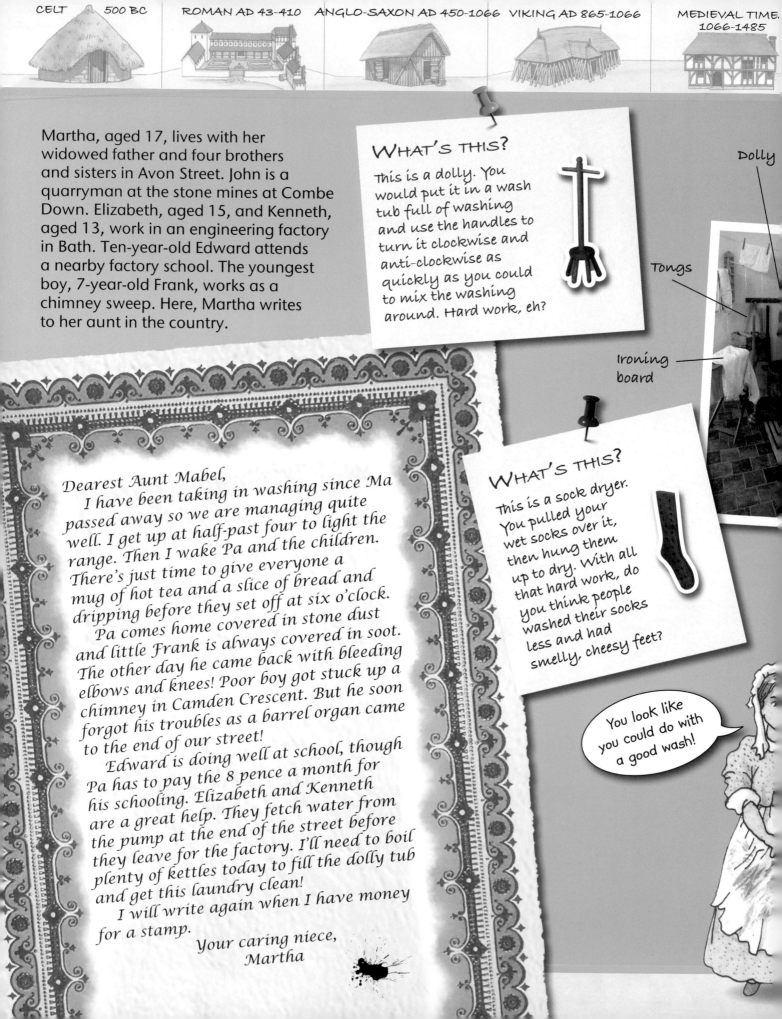

Martha, aged 17, lives with her widowed father and four brothers and sisters in Avon Street. John is a quarryman at the stone mines at Combe Down. Elizabeth, aged 15, and Kenneth, aged 13, work in an engineering factory in Bath. Ten-year-old Edward attends a nearby factory school. The youngest boy, 7-year-old Frank, works as a chimney sweep. Here, Martha writes to her aunt in the country.

WHAT'S THIS?

This is a dolly. You would put it in a wash tub full of washing and use the handles to turn it clockwise and anti-clockwise as quickly as you could to mix the washing around. Hard work, eh?

Dolly

Tongs

Ironing board

WHAT'S THIS?

This is a sock dryer. You pulled your wet socks over it, then hung them up to dry. With all that hard work, do you think people washed their socks less and had smelly, cheesy feet?

Dearest Aunt Mabel,
I have been taking in washing since Ma passed away so we are managing quite well. I get up at half-past four to light the range. Then I wake Pa and the children. There's just time to give everyone a mug of hot tea and a slice of bread and dripping before they set off at six o'clock.
Pa comes home covered in stone dust and little Frank is always covered in soot. The other day he came back with bleeding elbows and knees! Poor boy got stuck up a chimney in Camden Crescent. But he soon forgot his troubles as a barrel organ came to the end of our street!
Edward is doing well at school, though Pa has to pay the 8 pence a month for his schooling. Elizabeth and Kenneth are a great help. They fetch water from the pump at the end of the street before they leave for the factory. I'll need to boil plenty of kettles today to fill the dolly tub and get this laundry clean!
I will write again when I have money for a stamp.
Your caring niece,
Martha

You look like you could do with a good wash!

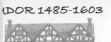

Here's how a typical Victorian wash room might have looked.

Iron

Wash basket

WHAT'S THIS?

This is a wash tub with a wash board inside. Bars of soap were kept in the wooden tray at the side of the tub. You would wet the washing, put it on the wash board and rub the soap into the washing by hand. Phew!

The Penny Black shows Queen Victoria on a black background. Stamps were printed on large sheets and had to be cut out with scissors.

R · ONE PENNY · A

PUBLIC RECORD

By Command of the Postmaster General.

NOTICE to the PUBLIC.

Rapid Delivery of Letters.

GENERAL POST OFFICE.
May, 1849.

The Postmaster General is desirous of calling attention to the greater rapidity of delivery which would obviously be consequent on the general adoption of *Street-door Letter Boxes, or Slits,* in private dwelling houses, and indeed wherever the Postman is at present kept waiting.

He hopes that householders will not object to the means by which, at a very moderate expense, they may secure so desirable an advantage to themselves, to their neighbours, and to the Public Service.

Not likely, Miss!

How do we know?

Life sped up for the Victorians. The new railways took them further and faster. Mail delivery times got quicker when the first mail train ran between London and Bristol in February 1855.

The world's first ever postage stamp was used on a letter posted in Bath by the city's postmaster, Thomas Moore Musgrave, on 2nd May 1840. The new stamp, called the Penny Black, quickly became popular, and within a few weeks the Post Office was printing 600,000 stamps a day.

The use of stamps brought about two changes: people started to cut letter slots in their front doors and postboxes appeared on streets for collecting letters.

CELT
500 BC

ROMAN
AD 43-410

ANGLO-
SAXON
AD 450-
1066

VIKING
AD 865-
1066

MEDIE
TIM
1066-

Bath at War

It's 11.20pm on Saturday, 25th April 1942. The first bomb has hit Bath. It's a clear moonlit night when around 80 German planes fly over the city dropping their deadly cargo. Firefighters, ambulance workers and rescue teams work through the night to rescue people and put out the fires. Another wave of enemy planes returns a few hours later – by this time Bath is ablaze so it's an easy target to find. Families huddle under staircases and in damp air-raid shelters, listening to the roar of the planes and the exploding bombs.

The 1942 bombings were called the 'Baedeker' raids after the popular Baedeker travel guidebooks.

Bombed Bath

During World War Two Bath became the target of two fierce bombing raids by the German air force. Hitler and his senior commanders chose Bath because it was an important cultural centre and they wanted revenge because Britain had bombed the medieval city of Lubeck in Germany. In just two nights over 400 people were killed, and over 19,000 buildings in the city were destroyed or damaged.

The Assembly Rooms were badly gutted by fire and one side of John Wood's Queen Square was almost completely destroyed. Oldfield Park and Holloway, where many families lived, were some of the worst hit areas.

At the start of World War Two no one was expecting Bath to be bombed. Thousands of government workers were moved from London to the safety of Bath. Around 7,000 children, mainly from London, were evacuated to Bath. The younger ones came with their mothers. The children didn't know where they were being sent. Most moved in with local families who had volunteered to look after them. A special Home for Bombed Babies was set up in Batheaston to care for babies made homeless by bombing raids – many of them were now orphans too.

The office where this book was made now stands here!

Do you recognise the Francis Hotel on Queen Square?

...1939 WORLD WAR TWO DECLARED...1939 EVACUATION BEGINS...

TUDOR
1485-1603

STUART
1603-1714

GEORGIAN
1714-1837

VICTORIAN
1837-1901

MODERN
TIMES
1902-NOW

Life in Wartime

Like other British cities, Bath was a very different place during the war years, 1939 to 1945. The huge Empire Hotel was turned into offices, and many other hotels, museums and schools were used to provide accommodation for the evacuees.

Streets, public buildings, shops and homes were 'blacked out' from sunset until sunrise the next day to avoid lights giving them away to enemy planes. Petrol was rationed so there were almost no cars on the streets. The last electric trams were abandoned in favour of buses, and the tram rails were ripped up and sold as scrap metal for the war effort.

Throughout the war, Britain's shipping was blockaded so food, petrol and other raw materials had to be found at home. People were given ration books, to make sure that everyone had a fair share. Allotments in Victoria Park and elsewhere grew extra food, and people had to reuse and recycle everything to survive.

Volunteers gave out second-hand clothing and toys to children evacuated to Bath.

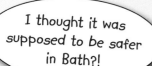

I thought it was supposed to be safer in Bath?!

TWELVE MONTHS' WORK

WASTE PAPER	1,045 TONS	This is returned to the paper mills to be pulped and re-used for munitions and industrial purposes. Light your fires with dirty, greasy or grease-proof paper which is not wanted for pulping. If you are not already a contributor ask your dustman for a sack and prepaid postcard
SCRAP IRON		
RAGS	442 TONS	Iron enough to make 177 guns
	34 TONS	Returned to Textile industry through the mills for the Army, R.A.F. Blue, khaki and export trade; some is used for munitions
BONES	28 TONS	Makes explosives, glues, fertilizers, etc. Bath school-children have responded well in their school bone collections
BOTTLES & JARS	150,385	Returned to Industry and Commerce
TINS	252 TONS	Flattened and returned to steel works
ALUMINIUM POTS & PANS	18 CWT	For war-planes. A gift to the Ministry of Aircraft Production
MISCELLANEOUS	20 TONS	Each plays a varied and important part in the War and industrial effort of the Country

YOU CAN DO MORE THAN YOU IMAGINE TO SPEED THE VICTORY!

CITY OF BATH SALVAGE SCHEME FOR
WASTE FOOD AND WASTE MATERIALS

This 1941 leaflet tells us how much the people of Bath salvaged over a year, including enough iron to make 177 guns.

How do we know?

During World War Two the people of Bath took their waste to special shops and street collection points – anything from animal bones to old clothing. Waste food was fed to pigs and chickens. Old clothing and rags were recycled into material to make uniforms for the army, navy and air force, while animal bones were used to make glue, fertilisers and even explosives. Many of the iron railings surrounding Bath's historic squares and terraces were removed and sent off to be melted down as scrap metal to turn into weapons.

Bath Today and Tomorrow...

We know about the history of Bath from what people have left behind. Written records, archaeological digs and sacred objects are just some of the things that help tell us about the past. But what will we leave behind to tell our children and our children's children?

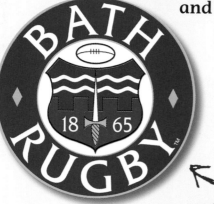

Founded in 1865, Bath Rugby Football Club is one of the oldest rugby teams. The famous ground is in North Parade. Do you think rugby will still be played in years to come?

The University of Bath sits on a hill looking over the city. Known worldwide for its excellent research and teaching, it is one of the UK's leading universities.

The first Bath International Festival of Music took place in 1948. Thousands of visitors come to the city each May to listen to music concerts. Do you think any of our musicians today will be listened to in 100 years?

I LOVE Bath! I just need a pic of the Circus and then I'm done!

Pulteney Bridge was based on a bridge in Florence. It was completed in 1773, paid for by William Pulteney. Will buildings like this still be standing in 2773?

...2007 THE FIRST BATH FESTIVAL OF CHILDREN'S LITERATURE...

Come on in, the water's steamy!

The new Thermae Bath Spa opened in 2006. It's the only place in Britain where you can bathe in natural hot spring water. The building may not be here in 100 years' time but chances are the spring will be.

Almost 4 million tourists visit Bath every year!

SPOT THIS!

Bath became a UNESCO World Heritage Site in 1988. A brass World Heritage plaque was fitted into the cobbles on Stall Street beside the Roman Baths and Pump Room.

How will they know?

Today's world of technology may mean that old written records are replaced with emails, music, even Facebook postings. Tourists take photos and souvenirs back to their homes all over the world, for future generations to see. Rubbish tips could give an insight into what people use and throw out. Will things in Bath today still be here for decades or centuries to come?

Bath has some of the country's finest buildings. Will these buildings still attract visitors long after we're gone?

...2010 BATH ATHLETE AMY WILLIAMS WINS GOLD AT THE WINTER OLYMPICS...

29

Glossary

AD – a short way of writing the Latin words anno Domini, which mean 'in the year of our Lord', i.e. after the birth of Christ.

Aquae Sulis – the Roman name for Bath. It means 'waters of Sulis'.

Bathon – the Anglo-Saxon name for Bath.

BC – a short way of writing 'before the birth of Christ'.

Bladud – a Celtic king who lived around 863 BC.

Canute – a king of England in the 11th century.

Catholic – a Christian religion that considers the Pope to be the head of the church.

Cholera – a deadly disease caused by filthy water.

Church of England – a Christian religion that considers the British king or queen to be the head of the church.

Curse tablet – a kind of letter written on stone, asking the goddess Sulis Minerva to punish someone.

Edgar I – a king of England in the 10th century.

Evacuate – having to leave your home and live somewhere else for safety.

Garrison – where soldiers stay while they are guarding a place.

Georgian era – the time from 1714 to 1830 when any of the four kings called George reigned.

Gorgon – a mythical monster with snakes for hair. It was said that anyone looking directly at a Gorgon would turn to stone.

Hillfort – a hilltop fortress built for protection, usually made of wood.

Hitler, Adolf – German leader during World War Two.

Medieval – a period of time in the Middle Ages: roughly from AD 800 to the 15th century.

Minerva – a Roman goddess of wisdom and healing.

Monastery – a place where monks live and worship.

Musket – a long gun, loaded from the front.

Offa – a king who built an abbey church and monastery in Bath in AD 781.

Parliamentarian – anyone who fought on the side of Oliver Cromwell in the English Civil War.

Quarry – a large place where people dug or blasted stone out of the ground.

Royalist – anyone who fought on the side of King Charles I in the English Civil War.

Scavenger – someone who collects rubbish and sewage.

Sedan chair – a covered chair with poles, enabling it to be carried by one person at the front and one at the back.

Slaves – any person who is owned by another. Slaves have no freedom or rights and work for no payment.

Spa – a mineral spring where the waters are believed to be good for the health.

Sulis Minerva – the Romans combined their own goddess Minerva with the Celtic god Sulis, and made one goddess.

...IN THE *1500s* TENNIS AND COCK-FIGHTING WERE POPULAR IN ABBEY GREEN...

Index

..IN THE *1700s* SHOP STALLS WERE SET UP AGAINST THE WALLS OF BATH ABBEY!

Acknowledgements

The author and publishers would like to thank the following people for their generous help:
the children of St Nicholas Primary School, Radstock; Dan Brown of Bath in Time;
Stephen Clews of the Roman Baths, Bath

The publishers would like to thank the following people and organizations
for their permission to reproduce material on the following pages:

Front Cover - Bath in Time; p5 Roman Baths, Bath & North East Somerset Council, Rachelle Burnside/Shutterstock;
p7: Bath in Time; p9: Bodleian Library, University of Oxford MS. Laud. Misc. 636, fol. 1r, Berig/Wikipedia; p10: Roman
Baths, Bath & North East Somerset Council; p11: The Victoria Art Gallery, Bath and North East Somerset Council,
The Charter Trustees of the City of Bath; p15: Courtesy of Özgür TÜFEKCL; p17: Bath in Time;
p19: Bath in Time (all); p20: London: B. T. Batsford, 1925 (A Dog Turnspit in a Kitchen at Newcastle Emlyn, South Wales
by Thomas Rowlandson. c. 1800. Source: Jekyll, page 43); p21: Bath in Time; p22: Bath in Time; p23: Bath in Time;
p24: 'Victorian Laundry' travelling museum display from East Sussex Schools Library and Museum Service;
p25: c/Shutterstock, Royal Mail Group Ltd 2010, courtesy of The British Postal Museum & Archive; p26: Bath in Time;
p27: Bath in Time, Bath at War 1939-1945 by David and Jonathan Falconer (Sutton Publishing,1999); p28: Bath Rugby
Club, Toby Farrow (Bath festivals), CIDPS, University of Bath 2010; p29: Andy Short/Thermae Bath Spa,
André Viegas/Shutterstock

All other images copyright of Hometown World

Every effort has been made to trace and acknowledge the ownership of copyright.
If any rights have been omitted, the publishers offer to rectify this in any future editions.

Written by Jane Walker
Educational consultant: Neil Thompson
Local history consultants: Andy Ellis and Dr Cathryn Spence
Designed by Stephen Prosser

Illustrated by Kate Davies, Virginia Gray, Peter Kent and John MacGregor
Additional photographs by Alex Long

First published by HOMETOWN WORLD in 2010
Hometown World Ltd
7 Northumberland Buildings
Bath BA1 2JB

www.hometownworld.co.uk

Copyright © Hometown World Ltd 2010

ISBN 978-1-84993-000-0
All rights reserved
Printed in China

Your past
Your now
Your future

Your history4ever

Mmm... Still love chocolate pudding!

Attention!

My next one's going to have 2 wheels!

Trophy for the trendiest glasses?

I love you too!